Loynton Mos

a natural and social history
of a Staffordshire Nature Reserve

What would the world be, once bereft
Of wet and of wildness? Let them be left,
O let them be left, wildness and wet;
Long live the weeds and the wilderness yet.

Gerard Manley Hopkins (1844 - 1889)
from *Inversnaid*

Staffordshire Wildlife Trust

Foreword

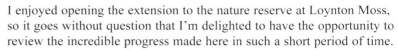

I enjoyed opening the extension to the nature reserve at Loynton Moss, so it goes without question that I'm delighted to have the opportunity to review the incredible progress made here in such a short period of time.

Peatbogs were and always will be my major passion. These hostile wetlands push human survival right to the limit, but ironically they provide an essential home for a unique range of biodiversity. Most of their species have evolved over time to specialise at living in these harsh acidic and saturated conditions.

My visit to Loynton Moss back in September 2001 brought back some wonderful memories from the 1960s of my time working for the Nature Conservancy Council, when I was based at Attingham Park. I soon discovered that there are few localities better to study these peatlands than amidst the splendid local Meres and Mosses.

These habitats have suffered their fair share of adversity, so it fills me with great joy and excitement to discover the extent that the Trust has managed to turn around the fortunes of this special peatland.

I'm under no illusion that the only reason that this site was saved from complete destruction was its designation as a nature reserve. Nevertheless, I like to think of this historical wetland as more than just an isolated nature reserve, it is and always was an integral part of the local area and community.

That is why I find this book so refreshing, because it recognises the important roles played by both its natural and social history in shaping the site as we see it today. This is a fascinating story of a wetland's natural development and the crucial interaction of local people. This turbulent tale 'ebbs and flows' all the way from the last ice age up until the present day. Long may its future flow.

David J. Bellamy

ISBN: 0-9549385-0-X

INTRODUCTION

Why a booklet?

The story of Loynton Moss is a tale of transformation. It tells of remarkable rural and industrial change as well as landscape evolution over thousands of years.

The Moss is situated next to the busy A519 - midway between Newport and Eccleshall. It's unlikely that many people travelling this road will have given a second thought to the unassuming countryside around Loynton and Norbury. However, further investigation brings to light a rich historical tapestry centred on one of Staffordshire's most significant ecological treasures. Staffordshire Wildlife Trust and Norbury Local History Group have joined forces to write this book especially to present the history of the Moss, and the Loynton estate at Norbury in which it once lay.

What's so special about Loynton Moss?

It is the dramatic physical change from being a large lake, known as Blakemere, to an extensive moss which now makes the site so distinctive. The relatively slow pace of natural change has been increasingly speeded up over the last few hundred years by human activity and exploitation. Loynton Moss is, nevertheless, a wildlife habitat and environmental archive of great importance in a region with too few such survivals from the distant past.

This book fits together pieces of an ecological and historical jigsaw illustrating a chronological journey from creation as a post-glacial lake to present-day site of scientific importance. Throughout this period habitats have altered, but the wetland has retained an abundance of wildlife intrinsic to the site, as well as a peatbed rich in clues to former land use.

The story is also about the impact of human activities on the Moss and how these reflect social and economic changes in local villages and countryside. Traditional exploitation for hunting, fishing and gathering fuel has been replaced by intensive forms of agriculture - both in and around the Moss. Nor was the Moss immune to the external pressures of the Industrial Revolution. Excavating the Shropshire Union canal in the 1830s had a lasting impact, trimming the eastern boundary and severing the outflow of water to the south from Blakemere to the Wood Brook.

The fall and rise

Most remarkable was the site's survival for so long into the twentieth century - through a period when numerous neighbouring Meres and Mosses succumbed to drainage and agricultural reclamation. This site's survival, like that of nearby Aqualate Mere, was undoubtedly due to the stewardship of a landed estate. Thirty turbulent years followed the break-up of the Loynton estate in 1969. Ironically, this event, which brought devastating consequences for the Moss, was just one year after the wetland was given protected conservation status.

The Staffordshire Wildlife Trust spent this time battling to sustain the wildlife value of as much of Loynton Moss as it could. Then, in 1999, came the first of three packages of grant-aid that allowed the Trust to purchase land which had been drained and cleared in 1970, and to develop an ambitious programme of restoration.

This book charts these dramatic changes and ultimately looks forward to what promises to be a positive future for this major Staffordshire nature reserve.

Some Simple Definitions

wetland: an area of soggy ground where root systems of vegetation are usually covered with shallow water

mire: a naturally water-logged body of decomposing vegetation solidifying into a peatbed

moss: alternative term for a mire in the Midlands or northern England, but especially one largely fed by rainwater collected within its own bounds

bog: a more widely used word, alternative to moss

fen: a mire whose rain water catchment area is much larger than its own bounds, and so may also be fed by streams

LOYNTON MOSS AND NATURAL SUCCESSION

Loynton Moss is one of a series of wetlands known as Meres and Mosses, found in an area linking Staffordshire, Shropshire, Cheshire and Clwyd. These landscape features are remnants of glacial action at the end of the last Ice Age. Huge blocks of ice broke off from retreating glaciers, gouging out hollows in the underlying boulder clay, and often being surrounded by drift deposits of sand and gravel left by the melting ice sheets. When these ice blocks eventually melted, they left water-filled hollows which today form the rich and diverse landscape of Meres and Mosses.

The current site formerly contained a lake of melted ice water created in approximately 8,000 BC. A large, steep-sided depression, known as a glacial kettle hole, extended more than 100 acres, gradually being colonised by vegetation. The open water came to be called 'Black Meere', or Blakemere, and was sustained by rainwater percolating through the soil within the catchment of the glacial hollow.

William Yates' 1775 map of Staffordshire shows these wetlands were once widespread throughout this part of the county. Unfortunately, many were drained for agriculture and others have shrunk in size due to the process known as *natural succession*.

Natural succession

The entirely natural reduction in size of glacially-formed lakes was the result of a peat-producing ecosystem evolving around the water's edge. Here, successive layers of peat were actively formed as partly decomposed vegetation, particularly sphagnum mosses, collected in permanently waterlogged conditions. This anaerobic process removes oxygen and nutrients from the slowly decaying organic material, creating acidic peaty soils. Each year a new layer of dead material is laid down before the previous year's has decomposed, compounding matters by sealing off oxygen to the lower layers. The process of accumulating slowly rotting material is excellent for preserving objects, effectively 'pickling' them - hence the frequent discoveries of ancient trees, animals and human remains in peatlands. These habitats are also excellent sources of preserved historical pollen samples.

Mosses, bogs, fens and mires

Moss is a regional term for a 'mire', a peat producing ecosystem which develops over time in saturated wetlands. Loynton Moss is the name now used for the whole of the Wildlife Trust's nature reserve. Previously, it referred just to the areas of fen and wet woodland to the west of the mere, which primarily consisted of Big Moss and Little Moss. Although commonly applied to such low-lying areas as found in Cambridgeshire, fen is a generic term for mires that receive water from outside their immediate boundaries. The name 'Blakemere' was given to the slowly shrinking area of open water which remained as the fen developed north-westward, circling a sand and gravel glacial moraine known as Rue Hill.

The largely wooded Moss we know today developed as part of this succession, producing a range of woodland, scrub and mixed fen communities. This naturally occurring process can have a dramatic impact on wetland habitats - particularly when exacerbated by human activities. Records from the fourteenth century show 'Black Meer' as a lake of over 100 acres. By 1800 it had shrunk to 35 acres. In 1920, it was only 5 acres, but still supporting a boathouse. In the 1950s the last true area of open water disappeared.

BLAKEMERE POOL

Robert Plot in his *Natural History of Staffordshire*, published in 1686, reported that "the banks of the Black Meer in the parish of Norbury doe yearly groe forward upon the surface of the water, three or four yards in seven years, the water standing under them".

The first useful map was a plan of Loynton estate in 1719 which showed that the total area of the Moss was 63 acres, with 'Black Meer' (the area of water) at around 36 acres. A sketch map of 1740, illustrating a legal agreement about the utilisation of water from the 'Meer', also defined the area as about 35 acres. It explained how that size was maintained by way of a raised floodgate installed on the outlet.

A sketch map of 1791, with notes by Thomas Burne, throws further light on the importance of this pool to the local economy. All three adjoining townships of Loynton, Weston Jones and Norbury had their apportioned areas of water shown, with a man-made outflow on the Norbury side of Blakemere feeding the stream that flowed into Coneygreave Pool. The water went on to fill the Manor House moat, and then lower downstream passed through a mill race in Mill Haft Wood.

The area of the Moss was recorded again on the Tithe Map and Schedules of 1839, which defined the area of the pool (water and bog) at just under 20 acres. By this time the Birmingham and Liverpool Junction Canal (now called the Shropshire Union Canal) had been cut along the eastern side of the Moss with considerable detrimental consequences. An estate survey of 1861 confirms these changes and shows that two-thirds of the Moss was classified as pasture land. The rest was water, planted with trees around the edge.

Although local rainfall was the primary source of water to the mere, the loss of its eastern catchment also included a significant supply of water from a stream which entered the mere from the east and exited the site to the north into a tributary of the Lonco Brook. The construction of the canal severed both this inlet and the outflow (through a culvert to the south) under the main Newport-Eccleshall road to Coneygreave Pool.

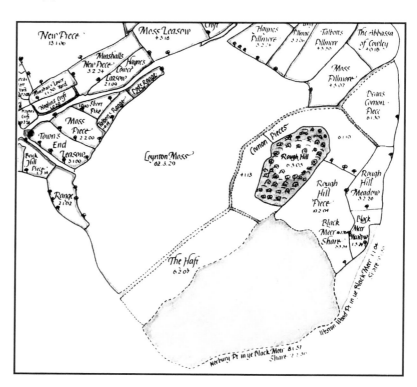

A section of a copy of the first map showing Blakemere drawn in 1719. It was headed with the title "The Ichnography of the Mannor House and outhouses together with a Mapp of the Lordship of Loynton belonging to Mr Higgins".

The Canal Company did not have the authority to alter or divert the pools and the stream supplying them. To protect the riparian rights at Blakemere of Thomas Higgins Burne, the then estate owner, a brick aqueduct was constructed some 25 feet above the canal. This 'water bridge', or Bridle Bridge, as it was known, had a unique double culvert, which was designed to enable a flow of water both ways. Interestingly, a new watercourse was constructed on the east side of the canal to take the stream water not required for Blakemere north-westwards into the canal. At the same time, to replace the former stream exit, a series of water steps was constructed a quarter of a mile south of the Grub Street bridge to deposit drainage water from the Moss into the canal.

Twentieth century restoration attempts showed that there were fundamental design faults with the aqueduct. The main problem was that the structure's arch was built too high, creating a slight peak at the centre of the bridge. As early as 1847, the Canal Company were forced to pay Burne approximately £500 for failing to complete the aqueduct culvert as originally agreed. Unfortunately for the Moss, the inflow of water from the stream was never replaced and this undoubtedly had a detrimental effect on the hydrology of the mere.

The excavation of the canal effectively created a barrier to the surface run-off and groundwater flow into the basin of the mere from the north and east. A hydrology map in the Wildlife Trust's 1984 Management Plan for the site shows that the estimated volume of groundwater flowing from this direction, and lost as a result of the canal's construction, was considerable. Almost ninety percent of its total catchment area was intercepted.

As Plot so exactly noted, succession visibly transformed the edges of the mere from open water to fen, bog and eventually wet woodland habitat. Local landowners before the nineteenth century had an interest in preserving Blakemere as a source of water, however, and seem to have taken steps to secure this. The imposition by Parliamentary authority of the right to construct a major canal to serve the purposes of far-off industrialists altered the position. This dramatically speeded up the natural processes of succession.

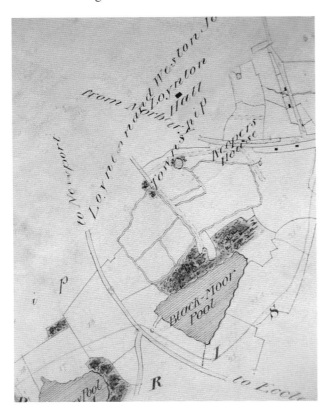

Part of one of the plans drawn in 1826 to support the Bill in Parliament for a canal through the Loynton estate. The surveyor was W.A. Provis, under Thomas Telford's direction.

A CHANGING LANDSCAPE - ENCLOSURE, DRAINAGE AND THE DISAPPEARANCE OF MERES AND MOSSES

Historical evidence from visitors' accounts, maps, field names and soil surveys shows that Blakemere was just one of several meres that existed in the immediate area around Norbury. Unfortunately, most of the wetlands described by S.A.H. Burne as "a Broadland in west Staffordshire" and which Yates' map illustrated so well, were drained and cleared as a result of agricultural 'improvements' in the eighteenth and nineteenth centuries.

Three meres survive. Aqualate Mere, near Newport, is the largest and is now a National Nature Reserve. Loynton Moss and Copmere, near Eccleshall, are the other two.

What became of the neighbouring peat lands?

Coneygreave Pool

Below:
Shebdon Pool with Offley Church in the distance, painted in the late eighteenth century.

Although not shown on Yates' map, Coneygreave Haft and Pool lay immediately southeast of Blakemere. The two mills at Shelmore received water from Blakemere Pool, via Coneygreave, until the Shropshire Union Canal cut off the supply in 1834. Construction

of the canal also claimed part of the pool, although the site survived relatively intact until 1969 when it was cleared and drained for agriculture by a new owner, Brian Dale. More recently, it has been reinstated under a Countryside Stewardship scheme by the current leaseholder, John Braithwaite.

Norbury

In his *Natural History of Staffordshire* Robert Plot recorded in 1686 an 'old pewit poole' about half a mile south west of Norbury church. This was one of the main breeding sites used by a colony of black-headed gulls called pewits by Plot. The pool had been drained by the time of Yates' map of 1775, but the 1839 Norbury Tithe Map shows five fields called Big Moor, Near Pool Place, Moor Meadow, Far Moor Meadow and Far Pool Piece.

Like the pool, the black-headed gulls disappeared too. However, Frank Gribble, as a much experienced naturalist, reported in 2001 to the North Staffordshire Field Club, that a colony had become established at Doley Common, Gnosall, some thirty years previously. Unfortunately, their breeding site was drained shortly afterwards, though a few pairs temporarily found a home in Norbury. Others could be found at Aqualate at the time Frank Gribble was writing.

Shebdon

The account of the pewit cull at Shebdon Moss Pool, vividly described by Plot, referred also to whole stumps of ancient trees found standing in the pool when it was low. The Commissioners for the enclosure of Shebdon started draining the pool and surrounding moss in 1811 - much to the anger of Richard Whitworth, the owner of the manor of Shebdon, who had not been informed. Whitworth's main grievance was that the water was being drained away to the south and not the west where it formerly fed his ornamental lakes at Batchacre. He also had a genuine affection for the wildlife of the local meres and kept regular diaries of the number of visiting black-headed gulls. Unfortunately, his suggestions that the pool should be retained as a fishery were ignored: the site was drained and formally enclosed in July of that year.

Woodseaves

Two pools were located immediately west of Woodseaves village. In between the pools lay an extensive area simply shown on Yates' map as 'gorse', but probably referring to a large area of peatland covered by bog, fen or heathland. Parish boundaries ran between the pools so that the eastern mere, known as Roan Pool, lay on Knightley Common in Gnosall and the western mere, known as the Pewit Pool, was located on Woodseaves Common in High Offley.

Both pools were drained in the early 1800s following individual enclosure acts of 1806 and 1822. Moss Lane now runs between the location of the former pools, and nearby is Gorse Lane.

Shelmore

There is some evidence of another possible peatland located at Shelmore. The 1839 map of Norbury Parish indicates a number of scattered fields to the north of Shelmore Wood with names such as Upper Mill Pool and Haft, Hernery Pool Piece and two Rushy Leasows. The name Shelmore probably derives from *scelf* (shelf) *mor* (marsh) - meaning wide, nearly level marsh. Thomas Telford certainly encountered huge difficulties in stabilizing the embankment of the canal during construction through this section, which possibly suggests underlying wet conditions or peaty soils.

One of the numerous granite boulders, known as 'erratics', originating from Scotland and deposited in the Loynton areas by glacial sheets.

The condition of the Loynton Moss site just before it was created an SSSI is well illustrated by this photograph taken in the late 1960s.

A cut section of the reed-dominated fen, looking north to the wooded canal embankment.

Insufficent groundwater levels have led to increasing encroachment from the surrounding scrub and trees. To try and impede this 'successional' process, the reeds are cut on a three year cycle, with one-third being cut each year in rotation. This prevents the accumulation of dying leaf litter and growth of young sapling which would quickly cause the reed-bed to turn into wet woodland. In recent years, sedges, such as lesser pond sedges, have become increasingly dominant over reeds.

THE SUCCESSION OF HUMAN COMMUNITIES

While the Ice Age kettle hole was changing naturally from Blakemere Pool to Loynton Moss, a parallel succession of human communities had the benefit of its watery resource. Archaeologists have traced Bronze Age people locally from their tools, though how these pre-historic people used the mere is speculation. The Romans built a road nearby, but no settlement has ever been found. Loynton and Blakemere Pool are within the parish boundaries of Norbury which had resident priests according to Domesday Book in 1086. Loynton was noted in the same survey, and these clues to Saxon villages are the first written evidence for the story of continuous human exploitation of the area around Loynton Moss.

In Norman times, and ever since, wetlands have been important features of local economies. Loynton was part of a feudal landed estate whose inhabitants worked the soil and managed its waters in communal fashion to feed and clothe themselves. In their agricultural economy, for example, they exploited the pool at Loynton for flax retting. This process, as a fourteenth century document shows, meant immersing the long fibrous stems of the flax plant in the waters of "the mere on the heath called Blakemereheth".

Flax production continued to be important even when other changes took place in the way the community worked its land. Robert Sharrock in the mid-1690s, writing about horticulture, thought Staffordshire to be exemplary in its cultivation of flax and hemp. That the crop went through the first stage of manufacture into yarn at Loynton is vividly shown by entries in late sixteenth century farm inventories.

Rushes and sedges cut from around Blakemere Pool could easily be taken to Norbury for thatching and house floor covering. Even when coal was available elsewhere in Staffordshire, peat continued to be cut for fuel as it was close to hand, and, for a long time, cheaper.

So long as flax retting polluted the waters, the possibility of fishing Blakemere Pool for food remains dubious. Plot, the first authoritative natural historian of Staffordshire, described the trapping of birds for eating at another pool in Norbury parish, and this may or may not have been done at Blakemere Pool. The process involved making artificial islands, or 'hafts', which Plot claimed were used to attract breeding pairs of birds to nest and rear young. The term was used quite widely for such platforms that were regularly cut and managed to encourage black-headed gulls to breed. An area within Loynton Moss has long been called The Haft.

Working large common fields in collective fashion was very evident in the fourteenth century at Norbury. These feudal practices ceased in the neighbourhood of Loynton Moss sometime in the sixteenth century at the latest. The estates within Norbury parish were split up into separate farms, often with enclosed fields somewhat scattered across the landscape. Blakemere Pool and its surrounding wetlands were located within an estate centred on Loynton Hall and first mapped in 1719. It's probable that farmers and other villagers had full access to Blakemere Pool at this time, but had their feudal rights subsequently unsuccessfully challenged. A mid-eighteenth century sketch map survives which shows how the waters of the pool were shared out between Loynton township, Weston Wood, and Norbury township.

Despite this, in the course of time, the lands and waters of the Loynton estate became exclusive

Snipe
The Moss was once a haven for this species and habitat restoration should entice this wader back.

property. The pool and marshy surrounds were reserved for the sporting and leisure activities of the gentry family at the Hall. For example, their nineteenth century Game Books are ample testimony of the wildlife they and their guests shot. Mr T. Collins, the headmaster of Newport Grammar School, no mean shot himself, but a bit shaky in his geography, wrote in 1905 that Blakemere was

"... one of the wildest and most sporting places in Shropshire. The pool is nearly grown up with weed. All round it is a sort of Indian jungle, which is always a sure find for a fox, and makes it a favourite draw for the hounds. There's always a fair sprinkling of pheasants round the pool, while on it are always ducks of various kinds. I have also seen as many as 200 snipe on the wing there at once. ... On one occasion a sportsman came down from London for a day's shooting. He appeared in the morning in patent leather shoes. At the end of the day he entered the pool and came out, but his patent leathers remain there still."

The cessation of traditional management techniques, such as reed cutting around the mere to encourage game birds, no doubt contributed to the build-up of vegetative material and consequently even more rapid succession. However, systematic cultivation of the Moss was not attempted until over half way through the twentieth century. It was moves towards intensified agriculture, in an era of industrial farming, which so alarmed the Wildlife Trust that it took action to reverse the process of centuries.

FLAX

Flax is an adaptable plant that, along with hemp, has been grown in many places. Several field names in Norbury reflect their former use for these purposes - Flaxpiece and Hempbutt being two.

The plants produce stem, or bast, fibres. These run from the root of the plant to the tip. Flax is grown to manufacture linen cloth and hemp to produce fibres for ropes. The transformation from plant to thread was a cottage industry.

Sowing the seed densely encouraged long, straight growth with as few side shoots as possible. Sowing was undertaken in the spring and the plants harvested three or four months later. The stalks were pulled by hand, tied up into bundles or beets and then stooked to dry.

To separate the fibres from the plant it was necessary to decompose the outermost woody matter. This was done by dew-retting: laying the beets out on the ground and allowing the dew to break down the fibres over 20-30 days. If the weather was fine and dry, this was hard to achieve. The alternative method, which appears to have been utilised around the Moss, was to water-ret. The beets of flax were submerged in pools of water for ten to fourteen days. The by-product of the process was polluted water, accompanied by a stinking smell. The workers must have been very unpopular in the locality. After decomposition, the fibres were completely dried and could be 'dressed', which entailed breaking the fibres with a mallet and then removing the broken straw. The flax was now ready to be distributed for spinning and weaving.

William Parton's inventory 1585

It in Beddinge sheetes [longer] sheetes bags
napiware w[i]th a cubbord coffars and all
Things to them belonging   xxvi^s vii^d
It 2 hatchelles & a payre of combes stoles
bordes formes trestells sythes an axe [agowrg]
a pickerell a bill & hatchet [& a garv on[e]]
chesell a spokeshave an aze a payre of vnges
a Bradsett a fringe panne & a hope a baskitt &
syves   xiiii^s iiii^d
It 1 wayne 1 plowye yockes 2 cheanes suck & Culter
1 harrowe 2 muck evells w[i]th all implements of husbandry   xxvi^s
It hempe & flax growing & in the house
3 Reaping hookes & his apparell   x^s
Some total   xx^{li} vii^s ii^d

This view of the bridle way, as it was in 2003, looks east towards Rue Hill with Big Moss on the left. It is possibly an ancient trackway known as Moss Lane, though very little of it appears on the 1719 estate map.

A measure of change over the last thirty years may be found by comparing this view with that inserted below. This shows a new drain dug during the clearances in 1970 immediately to the right of the bridle way.

A HARVEST OF PEWITS

The meres of Staffordshire inevitably attracted wildfowl to feed and breed. The most detailed description of the way people in earlier ages took advantage of migratory birds settling in these shallow waters was given by Robert Plot in 1686. He was told by the Skrymsher family, then the manorial lords of Norbury, that 'pewits' regularly bred on the pools of their estates, and not in those of any of their neighbours. Catching them in nets was an annual sport, and a source of delicacies for the table.

Plot included an engraving in his book which neatly illustrated the manner of driving the nesting birds out from the 'hafts', or islands of reeds, which had been constructed to attract them. Entangled in nets they could be killed or despatched alive to be fattened up and prepared for the table in gentry households often at a great distance.

M Burghers delin. et sculp

"But the strangest whole-footed water fowle that frequents this County is the *Larus cinereus Ornithologi*, the *Larus cinereus tersius Aldrovandi*, and the *Cepphus of Gefner and Turner*; in some Counties call'd black-cap, in others the Sea-or Mire-Crow, here the pewit; which being of the migratory kind, come annually to certain pooles in the Estate of the right Worshipfull Sr. Charles Skrymsher Knight to build and breed, and to no other Estate in, or neer the County, but of this family, to which they have belong'd ultra hominum memoriam, and never moved from it, though they have changed their station often. They anciently came to the old Pewit poole above mention'd, about 1/2 a mile S.W. of Norbury Church, but it being their strange quality (as the whole Family will tell you, to whom I refer the Reader for the following relation) to be disturb'd and remove upon the death of the head of it, as they did within memory, upon the death of James Skrymsher Esq.; to Offley-Moss near Woods-eaves, which Moss though containing two Gentlemans lands, yet (which is very remarkable) the Pewits did discern betwixt the one and the other, and build only on the Land of the next heir John Skrymsher Esq; so wholly are they addicted to this family.

*The black-headed gull, here on its nest,
is the bird Plot called a pewit.*

At which Moss they continued about three years, and then removed to the old pewit poole again, where they continued to the death of the said John Skrymsher Esq; which happening on the Eve to our Lady-day, the very time when they are laying their Eggs, yet so concern'd were they at this Gentlemans death, that notwithstanding this tye of the Law of Nature, which has ever been held to be universal and perpetual, they left their nest and Eggs; and though they made some attempts of laying again at Offley-Moss, yet they were still so disturb'd that they bred not at all that year. The next year after they went to Aqualat, to another Gentlemans estate of the same family (where though tempted to stay with all the care imaginable) yet so continued there but two years, and then returned again to another poole of the next heir of John Skrymsher deceas'd, call'd Shebden poole in the parish of High Offley where they continue to this day, and seem to be the propriety, as I may say (though a wild-fowle) of the right Worshipfull Sr. Charles Skrymsher Knight, their present Lord and master."

(Robert Plot *Natural History of Staffordshire*)

LOYNTON MOSS A SITE OF SPECIAL SCIENTIFIC INTEREST

Nature conservation value recognized

Amateur naturalists had taken a keen interest in Loynton Moss long before it was threatened with conversion to arable land. S.A.H. Burne, who died in 1972, while its owner, encouraged this as a leading member of the North Staffordshire Field Club. Many of the Wildlife Trust's founder members, such as Frank Gribble and Richard Warren, regularly visited the site during the 1960s to monitor the wetland's range of birds and invertebrates respectively.

The Moss was also the location for Kenneth Randall's field study in 1968 to examine the site's peat deposits. Randall, as a student of biology and a member of the Trust, was principally analysing pollen samples preserved in the peat layers. His study involved cutting two transects across the marsh and excavating a number of trial pits. One of these can still be seen today in The Haft, close to the wooden bridge.

This study was important in establishing the depths and location of the peat and mineral soils, and thus the initial area of the mere. Amongst his various findings, he estimated that the depth of water in the mere had originally been over seven and a half metres. The subsequent deposition of vegetation was clearly quite extensive as he calculated the maximum depth of peat at the centre of the Moss was approximately seven metres and about three to four metres around the edge of the former mere. It was also Kenneth Randall who first proposed the theory that, originally, there may have been two mere basins, separated by a mineral ridge of sand and gravel between Big and Little Moss, now used as a bridleway.

The Moss was formally recognized as a significant area for conservation in March 1968 when 95 acres within the Loynton Hall estate was designated as a Site of Special Scientific Interest (SSSI). This statutory designation was awarded by the Nature Conservancy Council (NCC - English Nature's predecessor) under the 1949 Countryside Act. Despite its considerable wildlife importance, this legislation was not strongly applied in practice as a conservation measure. Demands for agricultural and forestry improvements in the post-war period generally took precedence over the protection of wildlife sites.

In order to safeguard the site, the newly formed Staffordshire Trust for Nature Conservation (now the Staffordshire Wildlife Trust) started private negotiations with the owner, Colonel Morris, with a view to purchasing the entire Moss as its first ever nature reserve. Sadly, Colonel Morris died in December 1967, before negotiations were completed. Circumstances then required his widow to put this part of the estate up for auction at Newport in May 1969.

The Trust went to the auction with £4,000 - a considerable sum for the fledgling charity. However, Brian Dale of Dale Farm Ltd outbid the Trust with an offer of £7,000. Ironically, it was only by chance that Dale found out about the sale when briefly staying on his neighbouring property at Knightley Grange. He went to the auctioneers for the details and was informed that the sale was scheduled for that same afternoon. He made a hurried tour of the Moss and arrived back at the sale-room late, after the sale had already started!

Next day, the Trust Chairman, Phil Drabble, a friend and neighbour of Dale's, was having lunch with him and asked if he would sell the Trust part of the Moss. Dale agreed, but only 34

Kenneth Randall on Loynton Moss 1970

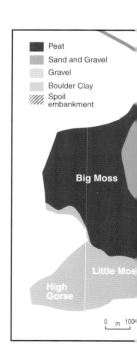

Peat
Sand and Gravel
Gravel
Boulder Clay
Spoil embankment

Big Moss

Little Moss

High Gorse

0   m   100

The destruction of wildlife habitats in 1970, so evident here at Loynton Moss, followed a pattern Brian Dale had set elsewhere in the county by clearing, for example, the medieval deer park at Bagot's Park.

He stipulated that a metal marker post be installed and maximum summer water levels in the Moss should not come higher than a point marked six foot below the top of the post - set at 107.3m ordnance datum. The post can still be found at the bottom of the canal embankment, next to Engineers' Pool. Its longevity is testimony to the arduous installation by Frank Gribble - hence its modern description as the Gribble post!

A new six-foot ditch was excavated around the edge of the remaining moss and existing ditches deepened. These were designed to receive water from the extensive system of land drains and to take water away from the peaty soils as quickly as possible. The clearance and drainage of most of the western catchment area now meant that virtually no groundwater was reaching the surviving area of moss in the care of the Trust. Another consequence was that an eel trap at the corner of The Haft was buried.

Soils of Loynton Moss

N

Hill

Rue Hill Slang

Loynton Moss

Stacey's Moss

acres and not the 55 acres that the Trust wanted. This included The Haft and reed bed areas, but not the important raised bog on Little Moss. Nevertheless, this was sufficient to allow the Trust to create its first nature reserve.

Dale began work on clearing trees from the major part of the SSSI during the following winter under a felling licence quickly obtained from the Forestry Commission. Most of the trees were bulldozed and burnt, though in some places the peat was so wet that it was impossible for vehicles to remove the trunks, so they were literally rammed into the peat. Following one failed attempt, an intricate system of land drains was installed in the peaty soils. Within two years of purchase the site was unrecognizable and already quite intensively used to grow a variety of arable crops.

Whilst the clearance was being carried out, Frank Gribble, a Trust council member, marked out the boundary of the Trust's land with binder twine. White paint was also used to mark trees at eye level so that the bulldozer drivers could see the new boundary. In order to prevent the surviving moss flooding the newly cleared areas, Dale set a restrictive condition in the sale to prevent excessive water levels on the Moss.

A losing battle

The Trust spent the next 30 years battling to maintain the wildlife interest of the Moss. In 1971, Kenneth Randall, in his capacity as Colonel of the 125th Staffordshire Field Support Squadron (Royal Engineers) of the Territorial Army, and his men, were particularly helpful when they endeavoured to repair the aqueduct sluice. Colonel Randall was well aware of the problems of the site from his earlier field study in 1968. His engineering unit constantly looked out for projects on which to practise skills, and in October 1968 he suggested that his squadron was ideally suited to the task of enhancing the water level of the Moss.

Various permissions were obtained, and in summer 1970 the squadron began work. They were part-time soldiers and the project was

Devastation

Frank Gribble painted lines on trees marking the boundary of the nature reserve and installed the water-level measuring post. In the surrounding area new ditches drained the peatbeds, trees were eradicated and a naturalists' paradise was ruined.

A vast range of invertebrates such as the broad-bodied chaser (Libellula depressa) disappeared; the ringlet butterfly colony on Stacey's Meadow was destroyed; bog rosemary died out, and several bird species such as redpoll, pied flycatcher, redstart and tree pipit lost their habitat. The most noticeable losses amongst the many species recorded by Richard Warren have been the disappearance of once highly visible examples such as the white letter hairstreak butterfly.

tackled at weekends. Over a period of about eight weeks 80 men camped in the field between Pool House Farm and the canal, with easy access westwards over the footbridge.

The Territorial Army team at work.

Initially the aim was to restore open water on the Moss, and high explosive was used to blow a hole in the reed-bed. This was expensive and ineffective. An experiment proved that after the explosion the fall-out simply returned to earth, more or less where it had been before. The second try was to use low explosive, but similar problems occurred. The third method was to construct a drag line - two posts with a line suspended between, with a bucket attached which was machine driven. This was abandoned as too expensive and time-consuming.

Eventually, it was decided that if more water could be diverted into the Moss, nature would do the rest. Consequently, work repairing the derelict aqueduct bridge began. Concrete slabs were made to create a walkway and to protect the aqueduct that had originally run across the bridge. To the west, ditches were dug and manufactured culverts were laid to ease the flow of water. Having done water-level studies for his degree, Colonel Randall knew that there was a design fault within the aqueduct. He was also aware that the stream to the north-east, which was to be used to rehydrate the Moss,

was possibly lower than the aqueduct. So, in order to raise the stream level, they constructed a sluice to control the water, and diverted the stream back through its original course, directly to the aqueduct.

So, the legend of the Engineers' Pool is founded on fact. Royal Engineers did travel regularly from their Meir base, improved the water levels, boosted their expertise and enjoyed the hospitality of the Woodseaves inns!

Unfortunately, the benefits were short-lived as the sluice created an excessive rise in water levels on its upstream side that proved intolerable to the local farmer. Furthermore, British Waterways claimed that, when in use, water was leaking into the fabric of the aqueduct and damaging it. The sluice was subsequently removed and the Moss continued to dry out at an alarming rate.

The same structural problems that hampered the Territorial Army's attempts to re-instate the aqueduct also blighted a hydraulic ram, which was installed by the Trust in 1993. This expensive installation quickly proved unsuccessful and failed to bring in a much-needed supply of water to the Moss.

The warm and dry summers of the mid-1990s visibly exacerbated the dehydration of the Moss, and even led to large cracks appearing within the peat in The Haft. In November 1996, the Trust joined forces with English Nature in a truly mammoth effort to control scrub and trees encroaching on the fen. This had the effect of restoring a large open area of reed-bed, but, without adequate water levels, this work would prove to be futile.

Ongoing management

The last remaining open section of the Moss was now the reed-bed below the canal embankment, overlying the final area of Blakemere's open water. By 1987, the Wildlife Trust estimated that more than fifty percent of the fen had been lost to willow scrub and birch woodland since 1970. It was deemed essential to maintain this final area of open wetland habitat in order to conserve the many surviving associated species of wildlife.

With the considerable help of volunteers, one third of the reed-bed has been cut each year since 1992, effectively cutting the whole reed-bed on a three-year cycle. Because of the naturally damp conditions, this is an incredibly laborious operation, as the reeds have to be cut and cleared by hand. What takes most time and effort in this operation is raking, removing and burning the cut vegetation.

Nevertheless, the cutting regime has been crucial in maintaining the last vestige of ancient fen habitat, an ecology which has existed for thousands of years around the mere. In the absence of sufficient groundwater levels, the dry conditions and build-up of vegetation litter would have quickly provided the conditions required for rapid succession to scrub and woodland.

Unfortunately, this cutting regime has not been able to prevent a vegetative change within the moss community. Reeds have been gradually replaced by a community of bulrush, sedges and continual proliferation of thousands of birch and willow saplings every year. The unforgiving summers of the mid-1990s made matters worse, and because of the increasingly poor condition of the reed-bed and invasion by scrub, there is regrettably no commercial value in the reed crop as thatching material.

Restoring sustainable groundwater levels has been the key to saving the surviving wetland. In the short term, only slowing drainage from the perimeter ditch and subsequently reducing the tree cover that had colonised the Moss would realistically achieve this. Despite owning the perimeter ditch (as part of the SSSI), antiquated land drainage laws meant that the Trust was not allowed to impede the flow in its own ditches. To exacerbate matters, successive landowners of the adjacent former SSSI areas were unwilling to enter any agri-environmental grant schemes, which might have countered the impact on crops from impeded drainage.

By the late 1990s, it was increasingly apparent that the only way to save the wetland was to obtain possession of the former SSSI area and therefore the right to reduce drainage. Unfortunately, meetings between the Trust, British Waterways and English Nature to agree plans to rehydrate the site ended in stalemate when British Waterways raised concerns that restoration of water levels on the Moss might de-stabilise the adjacent banks of the canal.

Above:
Lesser pond sedge which is increasingly dominant in the reed-bed.

Below:
The reed-bed in summer.

The road to restoration

Fortunately, luck finally turned the Moss's way in 1999, nearly thirty years after the site's almost complete destruction. The Lichfield Estate had acquired Dale's part of the former SSSI and, in negotiations with the Trust, revealed the prospect of selling 70 acres of land adjoining the Moss. A hurried application to the Heritage Lottery Fund (HLF) was successful, and, together with public contributions, enabled the Trust to purchase the 70 acres in 2000. The purchase included Big and Little Moss, thereby allowing the Trust to control water levels on the SSSI perimeter ditch. One of the Trust's first acts was to install a large sluice in the ditch on the north-west perimeter of the Moss to impede drainage.

This acquisition was quickly followed by a second when a 35 acre parcel of land at Rue Hill became available. More importantly, this land also came with the sporting rights to the whole Moss. The Heritage Lottery Fund again stepped into the breach in 2002 and agreed to finance this deal. The nature reserve now included 135 acres of land and, at long last, covered most of the Moss as defined by the pre-1970 boundaries.

Finally, in 2002, the Trust successfully secured capital funding from Ibstock Environmental Trust for restoration costs. This will enable the Trust to restore this wetland nature reserve to something approaching its former glory. A project officer, Paul Candlin, was appointed to kick-start the ambitious restoration project.

Bottom Right:
Tawny Owl - a breeding resident whose familar call is regularly heard during early evening.

Development of Loynton Moss Nature Reserve

- Original nature reserve
- 2000 Extension
- 2002 Extension
- ▨ British Waterways embankment

N

Far Piece

Rue Hill

Big Moss

The Slang

The Haft

Fen

Little Moss

Alder Carr

High Gorse

Stacey's Moss

High Bridge

A519

THE LOYNTON ESTATE AND ITS PEOPLE

Owners

Loynton estate and its resident owners at the Hall became the principal social focus of Norbury parish in the eighteenth century. The medieval moated Norbury manor hall, residence of the Skrymshers throughout the seventeenth century, fell into ruin and the family moved away. In 1775 Norbury manor estate was bought by George Anson, but neither he nor any of his descendants, the Earls of Lichfield, (who are the current owners) have ever lived there. Norbury Manor farmhouse, built near the moated site, was throughout the nineteenth and twentieth centuries either tenanted, or used by the estate bailiffs.

Loynton lands, held by Thomas Higgins from 1649, passed down the generations until Rev. Sambrooke Higgins died in 1823. He bequeathed the estate to his great-nephew Thomas Higgins Burne, of Himley in south Staffordshire.

Thomas Higgins Burne brought to Loynton a family which, by 1837, included twelve children. Their impact on the neighbourhood was likely to have been considerable. Certainly his eldest son, Sambrooke, had a local reputation, being described by a later family historian as "high spirited ... very irresponsible, surrounded by sisters, and having nothing to do but amuse himself, which he did by hunting, shooting and fishing." He died before gaining control of the property, which, like the family, had grown. When Sambrooke's son, Sambrooke Thomas Higgins Burne, took over his inheritance in 1874 he had around 1,500 acres compared with the 335 acres shown on the Higgins' estate map of 1719. At its maximum, the estate included most of the hamlet of Weston Jones, parts of Norbury village and all of Loynton.

During Sambrooke T.H.Burne's time Loynton Moss and Blakemere Pool were particularly used for those activities Victorian gentlemen considered 'sporting'. S.T.H. Burne kept regular and full accounts of all that was shot on his estate - rabbits, hares as well as birds - and he clearly set out to improve his fishing opportunities. Interestingly, he anticipated late twentieth century developments by installing a hatchery, fed by a spring, for breeding trout. In January 1883 a family memoir records that he received fish eggs which were successfully hatched by 23 February. It is not certain that he

Sambrook T.H. Burne and his family in the 1890s.

intended some of these at least for Blakemere Pool, for the same memoir noted that in October 1879 he launched a punt there to fish for pike "using bait from the canal".

After S.T.H.Burne's death in 1916 the estate declined, although his widow, Julia, lived on at Loynton Hall and was the last of the family to reside there. She died at the age of eighty five in 1942. It was her eldest son, Arthur, who was on the receiving end of complaints that the Moss and Blakemere Pool, by 1929, were "grown up a lot in the last few years and want attention from the sporting and other points of view." Arthur's uncle, Christopher, was the

The reason was that "there is no lying under these trees, and birds put up in that corner only give low shots or no shots at all." Christopher was old enough to remember the heyday of Victorian shooting parties on the Moss, and to have been told about earlier times. He pointed out to his nephew that "methods of shooting have altered since the old muzzle loading days but the traditions of those days still hang about Blakemere Pool."

The role of the owners of Loynton Hall in the parish as a whole was important, and their link to St. Peter's Church, Norbury, was always strong. Christopher Higgins, despite being

Fishing on Blakemere Pool 1905.

DATE 1895	NAMES	GUNS	GROUSE	PHEASANTS	PARTRIDGES	HARES	RABBITS	WOODCOCKS	SNIPE	WILD FOWL	TOTAL	REMARKS
Sept 3	Plardiwick	4		25		2					27	R.H. Hargreaves. T.C. Cholmondeley V.W. Dickson & self
23	Wood Eaton	3			40	5	9			1	55	C. J. Morris. J. Morris & self
Oct 2	Woodcote (Chadwell)	4		11	38		3				52	J.W. Williams. T. Ward W.C.H.B & self
5	Edgmond	4		30	8	3	6			2	49	T. Collins T. Perry. W.C.H.B & self
16	Ellerton	4		11	20		2				33	Col. Mansfield V.W. Dickson C.S. Baddeley & self
17	Showell Grange	4		7	42	1	2				52	H. Rogers. H. Rogers jnr R.T. Mansfield & self
21	Calvington	3		5	6	2	24	duck (3)			41	C.S. Morris J. Morris & self
24	Offley Grove	5					156				156	V.W. Dickson Rev G.W.Dickson R.H.H. & self
25	Wood Eaton (Cowley)	4		115	5	21	128			3	272	C.J. Morris C.S. Morris G.B. Lloyd & self (Cowley Pits)
30	Mobberley	4		24	7	10	3			1	45	R.H. Hargreaves. S. Lancaster J. Morris & self

Published by A. Webster & Comp. 60 Piccadilly. W.

One of S.T.H. Burne's Game Books recording shoots he went to and the totals of wildlife shot.

critic, although he recognised that some work had been done "clearing the drain from the Blackwaters up to the eel trap between the Big and Little Mosses. The drain above the eel trap which has been cleaned a short way is not the one from the E.T. to the Pool down which the eels come but the one between the Haft and the pool side."

Rampant tree growth was another cause for concern, particularly one group "in the corner of the High Gorse and by the Moss Lane Gate."

declared bankrupt in 1759, was a churchwarden and he and his two sons were among the trustees named on a brief for the rebuilding of the church tower. One of these sons, Sambrooke, had been ordained in Eccleshall in 1757 and was instituted into the living of Norbury in 1759. He also became vicar of Sheriffhales and a prebendary of Lichfield cathedral.

Between 1865 and 1877 members of the Burne family were much involved with the restoration of the east window. In the previous century it

Loynton Hall in the Edwardian age.

had fallen into disrepair, and had been replaced by a smaller round-headed one. Some of the nine daughters of Thomas Higgins Burne sought to replicate the original and by 1875 had saved sufficient funds for the work to be done at the cost of £150. At the same time, the white-washed plaster was removed from the walls and the plaster ceiling taken away.

The Rector at this time was their brother Tom. He died in 1887. He left the advowson of Norbury living to his nephew Sambrooke T.H. Burne, who subsequently presented Rev. J. J. Lambert (married to his aunt Georgina) to the living. He remained at St. Peter's until 1913. After the death of Sambrooke in 1916 the advowson passed from the family.

The church contains a number of family memorial plaques: a handsome marble tablet to Rev. Sambrooke Higgins, and a stained glass window on the north side of the chancel. In 1924 a beautiful altar cloth, elaborately embroidered, was presented to the church with this dedication:

To the Honour and Glory of God and in memory of Charlotte Anna Burne this Altar Cloth worked by her daughters and daughters-in-law was dedicated August 1924.

In the churchyard there are two large family tombs, one for Thomas Higgins Burne and family, and the other for Sambrooke T. H. Burne and his family.

Estate workers

Of all those who were employed on the Loynton estate the Allman family are particularly interesting. Their name occurs frequently in a Burne family memoir and in Burne correspondence. One of the Allmans was a gamekeeper and the cottage where he and his family lived seems to have been the only dwelling house on the Moss itself in the nineteenth and twentieth centuries. He was there, of course, to protect wildlife on the Moss as a source of food for the table at the Hall, and sport for the gentry.

The first of four generations of Allmans to have worked for the Burnes at Loynton is believed to have moved there with them when they inherited the estate in 1823. In the end, the Allmans have outlasted the Burnes locally.

George Allman

When George Allman, estate waggoner, died in December 1939 at the age of eighty-three, the local paper recorded that he had worked on the Loynton estate for seventy-two years. The newspaper also noted that George's father, Richard, had been employed by the Burne family "for over half a century". When George

This aqueduct over the canal, also known locally as the Water Bridge, was given a new concrete slab flooring by Territorial Army engineers. This covered the water-courses which were designed to take water both into and out of Blakemere.

Main picture:
Broad-bodied chaser dragonfly.

Below left:
Alder buckthorn is the principal food source for the caterpillar of the Brimstone moth seen feeding below.

died he was survived by one son, seven daughters, nineteen grandchildren and three great-grandchildren.

The son was Richard (Dick) who was at that time estate gamekeeper, living in a cottage on the Moss, near Blakemore Pool. He remained in the job after the estate changed hands, and was the last resident gamekeeper.

The cottage was in the woods on the side of the canal embankment near Rue Hill. The site is where there are now, in the early spring, great drifts of snowdrops. Formerly there were as many primroses and bluebells.

Right: Dick Allman the gamekeeper.

The cottage was reasonably substantial, brick-built with three bedrooms. Downstairs there was a front room, kitchen, and wash-house with a copper boiler. Outside there was an earth closet and a pig-sty. There was a well, but certainly by the twentieth century drinking water had to be fetched from a house on the main road. Milk was got from Church Farm in Norbury, but coal was delivered by lorry - by the 1930s at any rate. Lighting was by Aladdin oil lamp (even Loynton Hall never had electricity in the Burnes' time) and cooking and heating done by a kitchen range.

Dick Allman's son, Charlie, remembers Squire Burne bringing shooting parties in the winter into the cottage front room to have their sandwiches and beer. Granddaughter Valery Payne remembers the home-grown vegetables and fruit, and all the rabbits they ate - and the are are still gooseberry bushes growing around the cottage site. Grandmother Allman used the rabbit skins to make rugs, having dried them in the washhouse.

Charlie Allman also recalls the times when, as a boy, if he was fishing in the canal when the chocolate boat (on its way to Cadbury's factory

at Knighton) came by, he would throw his cap on the boat as it came under High Bridge and then run fast down to the Bridle Bridge where he would get it back, full of chocolate crumb.

The gamekeeper before Dick Allman was Frank Cooper, and two of his granddaughters, Mrs Rose Beech and Mrs Margaret Oakley, both around ninety years old, were still living in Woodseaves in 2004. They too remembered visiting their grandparents in the wood, and the thrill of venturing near the pool, despite dire warnings.

The cottage was demolished in the 1960s, at the same time as Townsend Cottage, on Grub Street, where other Allman family members had lived. Miriam Allman, one of George's daughters, lived for much of her adult life in Rose Cottage, Norbury (an estate cottage) and is remembered with affection by a former evacuee who was billeted with her in 1940. She was at that time the village post-mistress. She is also remembered locally for having a very powerful voice which was always to be heard leading the hymn singing in Norbury church.

Bessie Allman, grandmother of Dick, is recorded in 1877 as one of the local women called in to help the domestic staff in the Hall with the fortnightly wash. This monumental event started on Saturday, was in full swing between 3 am and 8 pm on Monday, and continued well into Tuesday. Bessie helped with the ironing, for which she was paid one shilling a day.

That the Allmans were appreciated by the Squire and his family may be judged by the references to them in the letters and diaries that were kept and used for a Burne family memoir. The custom of acknowledging good service goes further back. In Norbury churchyard there is a tombstone dated 1864 for William Cliff as testimony to this high regard.

Tenants

On the estate the chief figures were the dozen or so tenant farmers, and an important date in their calendar was the day rent was due.

In 1851, the quarterly Tenants' Supper was described in a most evocative letter from Tom Burne to his brother. The tenants, having paid over their rent, were entertained to supper in the dining room of the Hall. Evidently it was the custom for various tenants to propose a toast. Tom wrote that "Tommy Norris" (who incidentally was also a clock maker in Weston Jones) "was very loquacious. He proposed the health of Miss Susannah (meaning Georgiana) Burne, because one day she went to Weston Jones with me and, as Tommy Norris said, "the Missus said 'Miss Burne, will you come and sit down', and her come in". After the toast, "up got Tommy again and said he had an health

to propose, it was the health of a lady who came down ('mind you', said he, 'I speak upon facts') and 'came one day into my house, my lonely cot, and sat down and nursed my youngest child. I can assure you, gentlemen, that I was as proud to see that child nursed by that lady as the child was to be nursed.' And he proposed the health of Miss Rachel Higgins Burne."

The tradition of women of the family doing charitable visits to the poor within the parish was carried on until the Burne dynasty came to an end; old Mrs Julia Burne was remembered until recently in Norbury for bringing food and sometimes medicines on her bicycle to people in need almost to the end of her life in 1942.

Above:
Bessie Allman and husband Dick.

Left:
Domestic staff at Loynton Hall in the 1890s.

An illustration of the nature of the relationship between the Burnes and their staff, their tenants, and their neighbours in the parish, is given in an account of a tree-planting ceremony in January 1919, initiated by James Booker, the estate steward. Three copper beeches in memory of three sons of S.T.H. Burne who served in the army during the Great War were solemnly planted in the lawn at the Hall, along with a double crimson hawthorn. Eight village boys were invited to do the planting, two for each tree, "so that the history and meaning of the trees might be kept alive as long as the trees." George Allman, Bob Turner and Tom Felton were from families resident in the parish for four generations. The Allmans were estate employees, the Feltons were Burne tenant farmers and the Turners (Derrington Turner) were freeholders, formerly tenant farmers, but not of the Loynton estate. Another boy mentioned, Tom Bray, was third generation. His family left the area in the 1930s, but he returned in the 1990s and died only in January 2004 aged ninety-five. Descendants of the Felton family still live locally. The Derrington Turners moved away in the 1920s, but retained land at Oulton.

Bottom Right:
Two War memorials at Norbury.

Below:
Lower Farm, Weston Jones, on the Burne Estate.

Norbury is unusual in that it has two war memorials for The Great War 1914-18. The first has the names of those who died, and the second is for those who served and survived. On both the names are listed in alphabetical order without any reference to rank. Among the names are two Allmans, four Baileys, one Booker, three Burnes, one Felton, three Tills, three Tilleys, and four Talbots. That thirty-five young, able-bodied men (approximately ten percent of the population of the parish) were away for a period of several years must have had a considerable impact on the local workforce.

The seven Servicemen who died in World War II are commemorated on a Processional Cross in St. Peter's Church.

Left:
The dog violet is found on the base-rich soils of the canal embankment which here enclose the waterway in a deep cutting.

Below:
One length of the canal towpath is included in a Millennium Trail laid out around Norbury parish in 2000 marked by specially engraved granite boulders all left behind by the retreating glaciers of the last Ice Age.

LOYNTON ESTATE AND THE COMING OF THE CANAL

Within two years of his inheritance in 1823, Thomas Higgins Burne found that two sets of surveyors were looking at routes across his property for a railway in the west and a canal to the east.

Both the railway and the canal proposals were intended to provide a shorter and quicker route between the growing industrial area of the Midlands and the ports on Merseyside than that provided by the fifty year old Trent & Mersey and Staffordshire & Worcestershire canals. Together they marked out the mid-1820s as a watershed in English transport history. On the one hand, the Birmingham & Liverpool Junction Canal (later absorbed into the Shropshire Union Canal) subsequently proved to be the last trunk canal constructed in this country. On the other, the Birmingham & Rock Ferry Railway was one of the earliest proposals submitted for what became the new-fangled transport network creeping across Britain. It was first announced in 1824, only a year after the final proposals for the Stockton & Darlington Railway were approved by Parliament. It is interesting to note that the railway plan was turned down, despite an amended submission the following year. The canal plan was accepted in 1826.

The route of the canal in the first plan submitted to Parliament in November 1825 was right through the middle of the Moss. There seems to be no record of Thomas Burne objecting to this, but it was altered in the final plan submitted in 1826. Quite likely the Canal Company realised the potential difficulties of trying to dig out a cutting across the bog and peat area. This was necessary because the canal was being built by the 'cut and fill' method to minimise its length, rather than following contours as previous canals had done. So the route was altered to skirt round the eastern edge of the Moss.

Work on the cutting was started in 1829 by William Provis, as contractor, and proved to be extremely troublesome due to the instability of the banks. It took four years to complete. Spoil was transported a mile to the south to the Shelmore embankment, which proved to be still more troublesome! Even before the opening of the canal in 1835 more work had to be done to stop slippages, and there were reports of further problems well after the canal was opened. Thomas Burne initially received about £1,000 from the Canal Company for his land, but there is a record of a further £1,100 being paid. The

The sketch map shows how Telford first planned to take the Birmingham and Liverpool Junction Canal west of Blakemere.

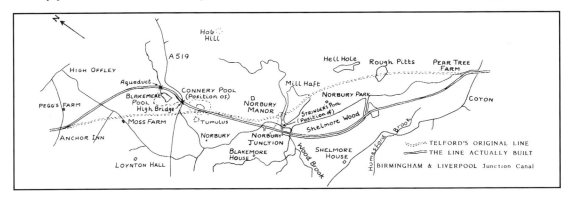

canal finally cost £800,000, which was double the original estimate. This overspend was entirely caused by the engineering problems encountered in the construction of the various cuttings and embankments, principally Shelmore, which alone cost £100,000! In mitigation, using 'cut and fill' was pioneering work and, as with all such enterprises,unknown problems had to be dealt with. This was cutting edge stuff, and soil technology was in its infancy.

The Act required that the construction of the canal should not interfere with any watercourse either into or out of the Moss. So an aqueduct was built to carry both inflows and outflows over the cutting. The Canal Company also had to pay the Turnpike Trust £50 to divert the Turnpike road (now the A 519) and erect a bridge over probably the deepest part of the cutting, some 36 feet above the water in the canal. It is less clear what happened to the run-off from the Moss, which previously crossed the line of the road at about the point where the bridge was constructed. It had drained into Coneygreave Pool on the Norbury Manor estate. There had been disputes between the two estates some years earlier about this watercourse not properly supplying Norbury Manor. Now a sum of £300 was paid to the Manor estate for loss of water, and a few years later Coneygreave Pool was recorded as being pasture land and remained so until recent reinstatement.

The Loynton estate was not slow to make use of the transport system that was literally on the door-step. For an auction on 4 April 1835 of trees felled on the estate a public notice announced that the timber could be removed by means of the newly opened canal. It had been, in fact, finally opened for through traffic on 2 March that year!

The prospect of a railway running through the estate caused concern again in 1862, when a proposal for a line from Norton Bridge (on the main LNWR line from Stafford to Crewe) to Shifnal, via Newport, was made. This was the period of 'Railway Mania', when all sorts of unlikely routes were proposed. Nothing came of it, and the only visible evidence of the proposal is a public house in Green Lane in Eccleshall, called the *Railway Inn* in anticipation of the line coming through, but even that was re-named *The Badger* in 1992.

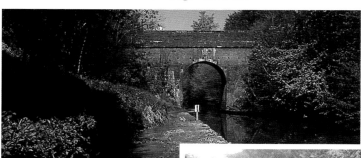

The construction of the canal in the 1830s brought a new type of job and employer into the district. Initially there were the several hundred itinerant 'navigators' (navvies) involved in the construction. They lived in camps or huts near to the work site, and moved on after their work was completed. The only evidence of their presence is in the church registers recording burials and baptisms (of children both legitimate and otherwise). They were followed by the canal maintenance workers who settled with their families in the houses built for them by the Canal Company at Norbury Junction, and have proved to be among

Below:
The Shropshire Union canal and aqueduct.

Bottom:
Frank Gribble leading a Field Club across the aqueduct in the early 1970s.

the most stable part of the community. Many were farm labourers who perhaps saw an opportunity for a longer-term form of employment than was available in agriculture working for a company rather than an individual. In any event, there are several examples in the twentieth century of canal employment running through three generations of one family. Of twelve canal workers identified in the 1901 census three of their family names are still local.

Aerial photographs reveal the changing landscape as between 1963 (below) and 1971 (right). The clearance of Big and Little Moss and the pattern of land drains installed there in close parallel lines is evident on the 1971 photograph.

WORKING THE LAND

The landscape around Loynton, and the Moss itself, has been shaped by scores of generations of people working on the land, as well as by nature. Changes in farming methods over the centuries have been the same as those elsewhere: common fields and wastes replaced by enclosures, artificial fertilisers supplementing animal dung, and tractors used instead of horses. Over a lifetime or two, change is often indiscernible. Any impression of stability in the rural community of Norbury parish is misleading, however, as a study of farming families quickly reveals.

True, a mixed agricultural economy has been the rule, but producing for a market has long since replaced mere subsistence as the aim. Inventories of farm stock and crops from Tudor and Stuart ages illustrate this well. These all mention cattle, some being oxen (castrated males) used as draught animals or food, but most were cows for milk and dairy produce. Horses were listed, but not as draught animals until the eighteenth century.

Half the inventories list sheep, which animals were important to the Skrymsher estate, for example, in the late 1680s. There was always a pig or two in the lists as well as poultry. Cereal crops such as wheat, rye, and barley were usually grown and there were references to flax and hemp.

Returns from Loynton to the Board of Agriculture in 1870 refer to a very similar mix. There were two farms, both over 100 acres, between them having 43 acres in wheat, 30 in barley, 27 in oats, 4 acres in potatoes, 26 in turnips and 4 in mangolds. Smaller areas had peas, cabbages and vetches. The practice of leaving land fallow had been dropped, but pasture land was divided between permanent and cultivated, 48 acres being devoted to hay crops. There were 61 cattle, including 20 in milk, and 283 sheep. Only 10 pigs were counted. There was an interest in dairy products shown in surveys of farmhouses just before the First World War. George Liversage, for example, used four attics at Norbury Park Farm as cheese rooms, and Norbury Manor Farm similarly had a cheese store. Loynton Farm, on the other hand, had a dairy but no cheese room.

There is still a mixed agricultural economy today, but the methods and practices

James Baker of Weston Jones: inventory of his possessions on his death in 1661. He had "one yoke of oxen, five cowes three heifers tow yearlings tow weeninges" worth £42. The oxen were for pulling a plough used to prepare for growing a cereal crop.

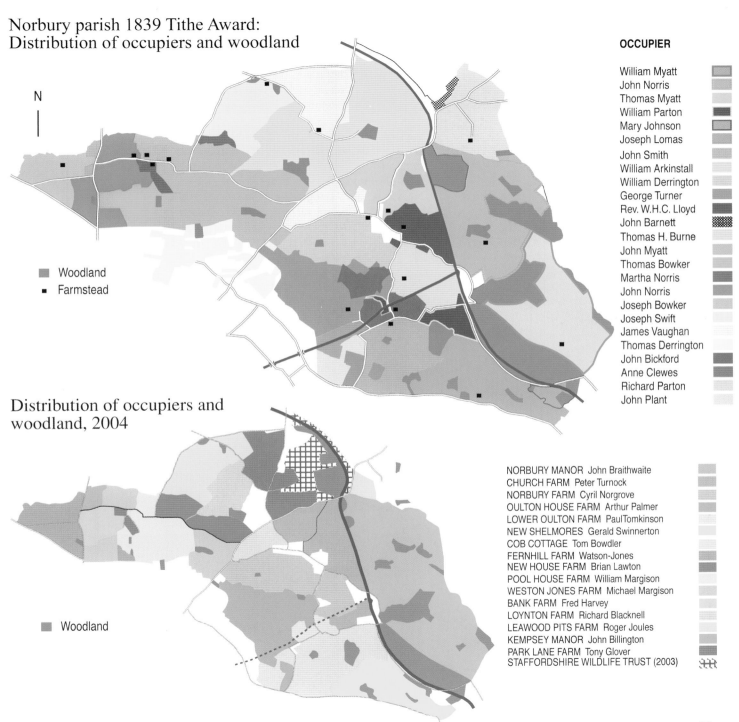

Norbury parish 1839 Tithe Award:
Distribution of occupiers and woodland

N

OCCUPIER

William Myatt
John Norris
Thomas Myatt
William Parton
Mary Johnson
Joseph Lomas
John Smith
William Arkinstall
William Derrington
George Turner
Rev. W.H.C. Lloyd
John Barnett
Thomas H. Burne
John Myatt
Thomas Bowker
Martha Norris
John Norris
Joseph Bowker
Joseph Swift
James Vaughan
Thomas Derrington
John Bickford
Anne Clewes
Richard Parton
John Plant

Woodland
Farmstead

Distribution of occupiers and
woodland, 2004

Woodland

NORBURY MANOR John Braithwaite
CHURCH FARM Peter Turnock
NORBURY FARM Cyril Norgrove
OULTON HOUSE FARM Arthur Palmer
LOWER OULTON FARM PaulTomkinson
NEW SHELMORES Gerald Swinnerton
COB COTTAGE Tom Bowdler
FERNHILL FARM Watson-Jones
NEW HOUSE FARM Brian Lawton
POOL HOUSE FARM William Margison
WESTON JONES FARM Michael Margison
BANK FARM Fred Harvey
LOYNTON FARM Richard Blacknell
LEAWOOD PITS FARM Roger Joules
KEMPSEY MANOR John Billington
PARK LANE FARM Tony Glover
STAFFORDSHIRE WILDLIFE TRUST (2003)

of working the land have altered. The balance between elements such as pasture and arable fields is different, and new sources of income provided, for example, by fishing pools are important features of a new industrial age of farming.

Loynton farms are part of a pattern of separate units formerly leased by tenants, with few owner-occupiers until after the Second World War. Maps from two surveys of land ownership and tenancies (the 1830s Tithe Survey and the 1910 Land Tax Valuation Survey) together with a special survey in 2004 for this book, give three nicely spaced 'snapshots' over the last 170 years of the pattern of farms. The two included in this book show that, while some tracts of woodland have shrunk slightly or been fragmented, generally land that was woodland in the early nineteenth century remains so today.

Woods were a managed resource, of course, as well as shelter for wild life. A nineteenth century entry in a Burne diary records men making clogs out of wood from alders, and throughout the ages trees have been planted, managed and harvested for fuel, building and for sale as timber. The 1836 Notice of Sale of timber previously noted shows how considerable this resource was. A letter in Burne family papers, written in January 1929, records that "the alders between the keeper's moss and the pool wanted cutting badly. They have got too big for crate wood, but they would make pit props or scaffold poles". It further noted "that there was a considerable amount of timber ripe for felling between the bridle and the big bridges".

Another continuity is seen in common boundaries between farm holdings, with many that existed in the early nineteenth century still

used today, despite the various changes in ownership and sizes of holdings. Groupings of fields worked from particular farmsteads could change quite quickly, but the number of farmsteads remained remarkably steady for a long period. By 1910 the Burne estate had become more fragmented with farm tenants increasing from seven to eleven, within a parish total of twenty land holdings above four acres. In 1870 there had been 21 farms and 25 were shown on the tithe maps of the 1830s.

Alder carr in winter.

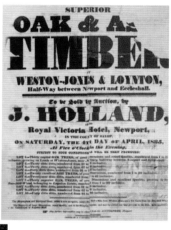

Timber felling is still a necessary part of site management.

The brown hare was among the first species attracted back to the Moss after the Trust gained control of the whole site.

freeholder. Smaller properties changed ownership, but there was still a high degree of tenancy. Nowadays, however, virtually all farms are owner-occupied. The exception to this is the Manor Farm which is still held by tenants of the Anson family's Shugborough estate, based near Stafford.

On the Burne estate there are examples of tenancies existing over several generations. One such was the Felton family at Leawood Pits Farm. They farmed there from at least 1864 until the 1940s. Tenants also became landowners. According to the Tithe Award of 1835 George Derrington Turner was a tenant at Oulton House Farm of Sir T.F.F. Boughey of Aqualate. His son William was born in 1839, and subsequently took over the lease, buying the farm in 1904. His wife, Catherine Jane, had died in childbirth in 1873 at the early age of thirty-four, but in the 1910 Land Tax Valuation Survey her Trustees are recorded as owning the farm, with Charles John, her son, as tenant.

Of the 23 farms listed at the beginning of the twentieth century there are currently seventeen. These are farmed by families who have subsequently come into the area, mainly after the Second World War in the late 1940s and early 1950s.

By way of contrast, (although not shown on the maps reproduced here for the sake of clarity), the size of fields has increased dramatically in recent years. This is the result of the mechanisation of farming, which has come hand-in-hand with the reduction of the farm workforce.

The road network shows very little change since the Eccleshall to Newport road was turnpiked in 1763. This by-passed both Loynton hamlet and Norbury village.

Although land ownership was predominantly in the hands of two large estates there were a few tenants of other landlords, and even the odd

A view westward across The Slang with Rue Hill on the right

CURRENT RESTORATION MANAGEMENT

Restoration of the SSSI

The nature reserve now consists of two distinct areas, each requiring very different management regimes. The first area, and most important management priority, is the surviving section of the original SSSI - that is to say, the 33 acres that had within it the most recently grown-over waters of Blakemere Pool.

Far Right:
The sluice repaired in 1971.

Right and far right below:
Volunteers have contributed a great deal to the success of the Trust. They have done, for example, much of the hard labour required to keep the reed-bed under control.

The ultimate management priority of the whole project is to restore this SSSI area to a *favourable condition*. English Nature define this term as "when habitats are stable or increasing in area" - in other words, are structurally sustainable habitats with long-term viable species populations and wildlife communities. At Loynton Moss the primary management aim is to maintain the natural range of key species on a long-term basis, and provide sufficient wetland habitat to support them.

A hydrological study during 2000 recognised the Moss's dependence on rainwater from the surrounding catchment area to retain its wetness. The drainage ditches installed around the SSSI and throughout the former SSSI areas in 1970 effectively intercepted the seepage of groundwater from its western catchment into the Moss. Not surprisingly, the study strongly recommended restoring the whole natural catchment area and stopping excessive water loss from the SSSI. The Trust immediately sprang into action to block the deep perimeter ditch with a large sluice.

Birch trees were cleared from the fen in 2004

A less obvious factor contributing to water loss has been evapotranspiration - water taken up through the extensive tree cover that had invaded the Moss. Pioneer tree species such as birch and willow will consume huge quantities of groundwater from peatbodies during the summer months. As drainage around the Moss created drier conditions within the SSSI, birch and willow seedlings quickly invaded and established themselves within the open fen areas of the Moss. With the slow restoration of water levels, it was essential to begin the first phase of selective tree felling, which started in 2003. This felling was restricted to sections of young birch woodland closest to the reed-bed. Just as in 1970, ground conditions made extraction impossible and many felled trees had to be burnt on site.

Monitoring groundwater levels is also a crucial element of management. Levels are recorded every month by measuring a network of dipwells that were installed with the aid of English Nature in 1996. Results indicate that there has been a slow rise in groundwater levels since 2001, but restoration of pre-1970 levels will take many years to achieve. One complicating factor to predicting future groundwater levels is the shrinkage and cracking of peat soils at Loynton Moss over the past 30 years. Once drained, peat naturally shrinks, but it is impossible to determine accurately how it will react to being rehydrated. As groundwater levels rise, there is even a possibility that as the peat absorbs water the ground level will also rise.

Habitats and species

The range of successional wetland habitats on the Moss can ideally be viewed from the Engineers' Pool. To the west, the reed-bed grades into the adjacent scrub, then into wet alder and willow woodland (technically known as 'carr') and on to dry oak and birch woodland.

Above:
A view of the reed-bed looking north from the alder carr.

Right:
The red hairy-ringed fungus Scutellinia kerguelensis on a tree trunk with the common moss Brachythecium rutabulum.

Wetland habitats

Although heavily degraded from drainage and encroachment by trees, the SSSI still retains many of the key wetland species and features that make this site so important. The basin mire is covered with a thin floating raft which has been colonised by fen vegetation dominated by common reed. For decades, groups of visitors have enjoyed the sensation of jumping up and down on the reed-bed to experience the 'bouncing effect' of a floating mat of vegetation over the lens of water below. However, once they are stationary again, they have an opportunity to discover some of the reed-bed's less common plants such as marsh cinquefoil, cowbane and branched bur-reed. More frequently encountered plants include greater reedmace, water dock and lesser pond sedge.

Crucial to the historical development of such peatlands and mosses are the *Sphagnum* mosses. The different Sphagna species are superb indicators of a site's water quality and quantity. At Loynton Moss this is reflected in the changing stages of seral succession occurring - from healthy open water and active raised bogs through to the development of fen, scrub and woodland. As site conditions have changed due to desiccation many of the true bog mosses have declined, whilst indicators of drier and more wooded conditions, such as *Sphagnum palustre* and *Sphagnum recurvum sensu lato* have increased.

The fen is fringed by a margin of grey willow carr that in conjunction with the fen provides superb habitat for a great range of invertebrates. In turn, these habitats and species attract many breeding bird species each summer such as willow warbler, reed warbler and reed bunting.

The area of alder carr forms a wonderful stand of wet woodland. The multi-stemmed stools arise from felling earlier in the twentieth century and, when flooded, this area resembles a miniature Everglades swamp. The prominent stature of these trees has been exacerbated by the shrinkage of the surrounding peat, caused by the increasing dehydration of the Moss over the past 170 years. The area still retains a relatively rich ground flora with species such as yellow iris, reed canary grass and white and tufted sedge.

The wet woodland also contains the largest stand of alder buckthorn in the county and other notable species such as bog myrtle, and

Bog Myrtle

elongated sedge. The bog myrtle is particularly important, as it is the last known surviving example of this species in the county. During the 1970 clearance, the last four shrubs were dug up from Big Moss and transplanted to the SSSI. Two further shrubs were also discovered within the remaining site amidst

the undergrowth soon after. Unfortunately, five of the shrubs (including the transplanted ones) died during the drought of 1976. The sole surviving bog myrtle has since supplied scions for new shrubs in locations throughout the county and several saplings have recently been raised to plant back on to the moss

The wetland habitats of the Moss host a whole variety of rare invertebrates. Some of the notable moths recorded within the areas of fen and carr have wonderful names such as the dentated pug, small yellow wave and the round-winged muslin. Unfortunately, the status of the dentated pug is unknown because its food plant, yellow loosestrife, is not as widespread within the carr as it once was.

Most of the other species do not have common English names, but are equally important and unusual in their presence at Loynton Moss. Money spiders, such as *Hypomma fulvum*, *Entel omissa* and *Porrhomma oblutum* are particularly unusual as they are usually restricted to wet habitats in areas such as East Anglia and southern England. Likewise, the harvestman, *Anelasmocephalus - cambridgei*, is normally found in limestone or chalk regions. Other rarities include the rove beetle *Schisloglossa gemina*, found in the dampest areas of the Moss, and the weevil *Thryogenes scirrhosus* found amongst the willow carr.

Yellow loosestrife

Common species of butterfly such as orange tip, speckled wood and holly blue can still be seen. The distinctive brimstone butterflies can also be found in abundance, particularly in proximity to their food plant, alder buckthorn.

Cinnabar moth whose caterpillars feed on ragwort.

Despite decades of dehydration, a number of dragonfly and damselfly species, such as broad bodied chaser and large red damselfly, have managed to survive the increasingly dry habitat conditions.

Visitors might not welcome the attention of the Moss's other prominent invertebrates - several species of mosquitoes. These insects are on the wing in sheltered parts of the Moss throughout the summer months, deterring all but the most determined visitors from entering the wetland areas.

Most obvious amongst the impressive list of 200 species fungi recorded are the elf cups in the vicinity of the site of the gamekeeper's cottage, and the *Birch polypore*, a bracket fungus growing on the birch trees within The Haft.

Woodland

The drier areas of woodland on higher ground support a very different flora from that found on the peaty soils of the Moss. The canal embankment along the eastern boundary was created from sands and boulder clay spoil excavated from the canal. Consequently, the soil here is base-rich and typified by trees planted or naturally regenerated such as wych

elm, sweet chestnut, ash and hazel. The woodland also has a distinctive ground flora with a range of plants such as dog's mercury, bluebells, wood sorrel, yellow archangel and buckler fern. The northern section of woodland is the best area from which to watch the magnificent sight of buzzards regularly soaring overhead hunting for rabbits over the open fields of the reserve.

Above:
Elf cups in a drift of snowdrops.

Below:
Buzzard.

The highlight of the canal embankment is undoubtedly the collection of glorious mature beech trees, which were planted at the time of the canal's construction. These are now in varying degrees of decay, but provide vital habitats for a range of wildlife, particularly saproxylic invertebrates and epiphytes (lichens, mosses, bryophytes and fungi) which rely on dead wood as part of their life-cycle. Unfortunately, many of these saproxylic species, such as the net-winged beetle *Platycis minutes*, tend to be rare as dead wood habitats are invariably felled before reaching maturity, or veteran trees and fallen timber are 'tidied-up'. Where possible, dead wood is retained on site at Loynton Moss to provide a continuous habitat for such species and the creatures that feed on them.

The other dry wooded areas have contrasting origins and ultimately are characterised by different floras. The woodland on the higher areas of The Haft has grown on peaty soils and has consequently developed a typically acidic flora. The main tree species are oak, birch, holly and rowan, whilst climbers such as honeysuckle and corydalis are also prevalent. Spring is the best time to see colourful plants such as bluebells, celandine and wood sorrel, as bracken and broad buckler fern tend to dominate the ground flora throughout the later summer months. One unlikely shrub that keen observers might notice is snowy mespilus or juneberry. This is a North American shrub that has somehow found its way into the woodland and established itself along the southern section of the circular path.

From left to right:
Sphagnum recurvum sensu lato and the flower of marsh cinquefoil.

Below:
A pair (male and female) of large red damselflies on celery-leaved buttercups, and the elegant Mnium hornum.

Maps indicate that the woodland on Rue Hill was planted at the end of the nineteenth century on a former meadow. Although heavily thinned in recent years, tall ash trees still dominate the woodland stand, though there is not a particularly rich ground flora. The main botanical interest is a colony of bluebells at the western edge, which is probably a legacy from the adjacent former old woodland cleared in 1970.

Perhaps the most unusual flora is found around the site of the former gamekeeper's cottage, located in a hollow just off the north-eastern corner of The Slang. Although only abandoned in the 1960s, the foundations are now covered in vegetation and scarcely discernible even to those familiar with its location. The main indication of a settlement is the profusion of snowdrops along the embankment every February. Other garden escapees include a number of vigorous herbs which still survive amongst the dense brambles and nettles. The cottage retained a small meadow at the eastern end of The Slang, but the remnants of this were destroyed in 1970.

Recreating lost habitats

The two blocks of land acquired in 2000 and 2002 now form the largest part of the nature reserve. The main priority for these areas will also be to assist in restoring water levels in the SSSI, by raising levels in the surrounding ditches. Furthermore, they also offer a wonderful opportunity to recreate some of the wetland habitats that were destroyed in 1970 and have subsequently become so rare throughout Staffordshire.

During 30 years of intensive arable cultivation, these fields received huge inputs of fertilizers and pesticides. Last harvested in 1999, the enriched fields were left fallow for two years

Right:
Breaking up the
land drains.

and predictably were soon producing massive flushes of weed growth. This was very attractive to many forms of wildlife, but not conducive to restoring the SSSI and even less popular with the local farming community. Inevitably, the Trust's first responsibility was to implement a cutting regime to control these aggressive flushes of nettles, thistles, ragwort and willow herbs.

Farming machinery was also brought in to break up the extensive system of land drains, which has certainly had the effect of reducing drainage from Big Moss and Little Moss. The Trust is restricted in fully restoring groundwater levels, however, as the levels in the outer perimeter ditch have to be kept very low to maintain adequate drainage from adjacent farmland. The hydrological survey was crucial, therefore, in identifying land-levels and areas for potentially raising ditch water levels without affecting the property of neighbours. Fortunately, the best potential areas for re-creating wetland habitats are on the peaty soils of the low-lying sections of Big and Little Moss, which once formed the early Blakemere.

Because of its former agricultural use, re-creating wildlife habitats will initially require extensive management to exhaust the enriched soil. One of the ideal short-term management methods to achieve this is to introduce grazing animals. The land having never been used for grazing, an expensive infrastructure of fencing, gates and water points had to be installed by the Trust. A number of management compartments have now been established, based on the hydrological study and former habitats. Big Moss is the largest of these compartments - a low- lying area with deep peaty soils, occupying the most extensive former area of the mere.

Raising groundwater levels and introducing low density cattle grazing will help create lowland wet grassland. This type of habitat is important for a range of wildlife - most noticeably wading birds such as snipe, lapwing and curlew. As groundwater levels are slowly restored, nutrient and phosphate levels will fall and different vegetation will develop. After this initial stage, it may be possible to partially restore or gradually recreate the former fen vegetation on this field.

The eastern section of Little Moss occupies another low-lying area. A similar management regime is being adopted with cattle grazing, though its close proximity to the SSSI should enable more rapid development of fen vegetation.

High Gorse, Stacey's Moss and Rue Hill occupy the higher ground on the mineral ridge surrounding the depression of the former mere. These areas will be managed to re-create an attractive mixture of dry grassland, meadows and scrub. Seed from the hay meadows at Mottey Meadows National Nature Reserve (at nearby Wheaton Aston) has also been sown into the fields to help increase the botanical diversity of Stacey's Moss and High Gorse.

Many once common farmland species have been lost over the past 50 years because of agricultural intensification and habitat loss. Within three years of the Trust's acquisitions, species such as hare and skylark were already re-colonising the site and there is enormous potential for traditional management to attract other important species of wildlife.

One remarkable tale is of the ringlet butterfly found until 1979 on Stacey's Moss, where its caterpillars fed on the profusion of sedges and grasses. It was then only reported along the road verge until 1983, when presumed extinct. In the two summers since Stacey's Moss was reseeded in 2002 the ringlet has been seen there again. It is assumed that it survived on roadside vegetation, but has now recolonised its former habitat.

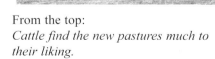

From the top:
Cattle find the new pastures much to their liking.

Hay was strewn on Little Moss in 2002.

Yellow Rattle.

THE FUTURE

The concealed and private status of this wetland helped to protect this site from the agricultural 'improvements' of the eighteenth and nineteenth centuries. Ironically, this seclusion ultimately contributed to this unique habitat almost slipping from the map without a trace. Thankfully, protective legislation is now stronger and attitudes concerning the natural environment have changed. Never again should we see such a catalogue of damage and destruction to part of our natural heritage.

Raising awareness and appreciation of Loynton Moss within the local community is a positive action that will also help safeguard against any future threats. The public is now actively encouraged to visit the Moss and learn about its history and value. Funding from a variety of sources has provided the Trust with the resources to develop an infrastructure of access and facilities. A series of footpaths is being created, new interpretation boards installed, a car parking area created and benches placed at key points. Ongoing community events and activities will enable involvement and interaction with local people.

Degraded and bruised perhaps, but unlike its neighbours, Loynton Moss has managed to survive into the twenty first century. It has overcome innumerable challenges and its future is at long last looking much brighter. Water levels are rising, invasive tree cover on the Moss is being reduced and the total area under positive conservation management has almost been restored to the 1970 boundaries.

Realistically, restoration work will take many years to achieve and will never fully re-create the open water of Blakemere or the peat body destroyed in 1970. However, the Trust's activities will safeguard the last remaining fragment of Loynton Moss for future generations, and enable the re-creation of many other valuable wetland habitats. The Trust's objective is the creation of a seamless nature reserve where wetland habitats merge naturally with each other in a catchment area with sustainable groundwater levels.

This is a long-term goal, and it is a realistic one. Moreover, the achievement of such a goal is vital if this wetland's habitats and associated wildlife have any hope of a sustainable future. This is the very least that this unique and special wetland deserves.

Summer and winter contrasted in the footpath from the Glade looking north-west, with yellow flag iris in the centre, great reedmace to the right and a broad-bodied chaser to the left.